KT-579-462

Middle-East

Phoenicians	Sumerians	Hebrews

Asia

Chinese	Japanese	Indians

c36 000 Primitive people in Lower Yellow River Valley

30 000 B.C. people hunted.

America

Mayas	Aztecs	Incas	First Americans

c25 000 — 17 000 B.C. Hunting people inhabit Canada, Mexico, Andes

c50 000 — 20 000 B.C. First migrants from Asia reached North America

---

Time scale (right edge, top to bottom): 8000 · 7500 · 7000 · 6500 · 6000 · 5500 · 5000 · 4500 · 4000 · 3500 · 3000 · 2500 · 2000 · 1500 · 1000 · 500 · 0 B.C./A.D. · 500 · 1000 · 1500 · 2000

Middle-East

Phoenicians
- Phoenicians settle (~2900 B.C.)
- Egyptian, Babylonian, Hittite influence (~1900 B.C.)
- Phoenicians trading in Mediterranean (~1500 B.C.)
- Carthage established
- Persians dominate
- Greeks take Tyre
- Punic Wars
- Roman domination

Sumerians
- Oldest inscribed tablet at Kish (~3300 B.C.)
- Ur supreme
- Hammurabi of Babylon rules
- First Assyrian Empire
- Wars between Persians and Greeks

Hebrews
- First pottery (~4500 B.C.)
- Semi-nomadic
- Abraham, Isaac and Jacob
- Egypt dominates
- King David
- Israel & Judah
- Assyrians
- Babylonians
- Greeks
- Romans take Judea
- Hebrew lands fall to Romans; Hebrews without homeland until 1948, when Jews given Israel

Asia

Chinese
- Hsia Dynasty (~2000 B.C.)
- Shang Dynasty
- Chou Period
- Civil wars
- Ch'in Dynasty
- Han Dynasty
- chaos and unrest
- China united
- Sung Dynasty
- Yuan Dynasty
- Ming Dynasty
- Ch'ing Dynasty
- Opium Wars

Japanese
- Yao period begins
- Classic Buddhist Japan
- Capital moved to Heian (Kyoto)
- Civil war
- Early Modern Japan

Indians
- Civilisation in the Indus valley (~2500 B.C.)
- Aryans invade
- Greeks reach India
- Greeks expelled
- Invasions
- Gupta Empire
- First Muslims rule
- Moghul Empire

America

Mayas
- Maya civilisation in Yucatan

Aztecs
- Culture in Mexico
- Climax of Oltec culture
- First pryamids in Mexico
- Aztec settlement on Lake islands
- Spanish under Cortes capture Aztec lands

Incas
- Machu Picchu built
- Inca civilisation flourishes
- Spanish invasions of Inca and Maya lands

First Americans
- Pottery in south-east of North America
- Eskimo culture begins to use sea as a source of food
- 'Mound Builders' inhabit Ohio Valley
- White settlers cultivate Virginia
- African Negroes sold as slaves

Columbus reached the New World

BM EDUCATION SERVICE LIBRARY

PHL

5406000021 3966

The Vikings

THE
**PAUL HAMLYN
LIBRARY**

DONATED BY

THE PAUL HAMLYN

FOUNDATION

TO THE

BRITISH MUSEUM

opened December 2000

THE ANCIENT WORLD

The Vikings

Pamela Odijk

BM EDUCATION SERVICE LIBRARY

WITHDRAWN

M

THE
BRITISH
MUSEUM
WITHDRAWN
THE PAUL HAMLYN LIBRARY

948.022 ODI

The Vikings

Contents

The Vikings: timeline

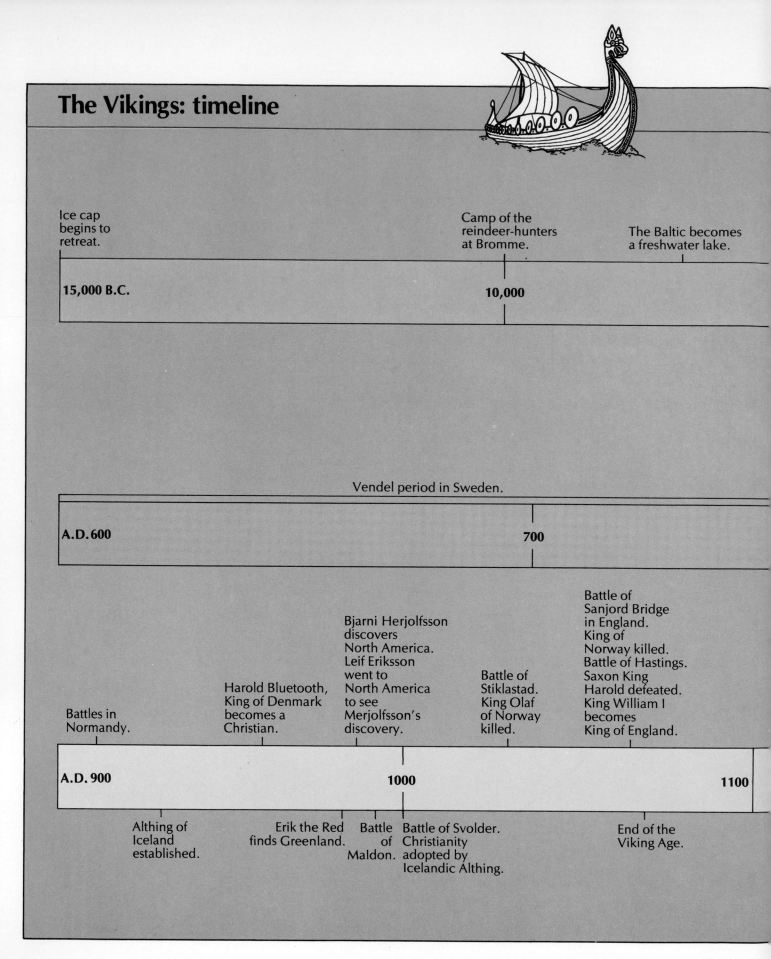

Ice cap begins to retreat.

Camp of the reindeer-hunters at Bromme.

The Baltic becomes a freshwater lake.

15,000 B.C.

10,000

Vendel period in Sweden.

A.D.600

700

Battles in Normandy.

Harold Bluetooth, King of Denmark becomes a Christian.

Bjarni Herjolfsson discovers North America. Leif Eriksson went to North America to see Merjolfsson's discovery.

Battle of Stiklastad. King Olaf of Norway killed.

Battle of Sanjord Bridge in England. King of Norway killed. Battle of Hastings. Saxon King Harold defeated. King William I becomes King of England.

A.D. 900

1000

1100

Althing of Iceland established.

Erik the Red finds Greenland.

Battle of Maldon.

Battle of Svolder. Christianity adopted by Icelandic Althing.

End of the Viking Age.

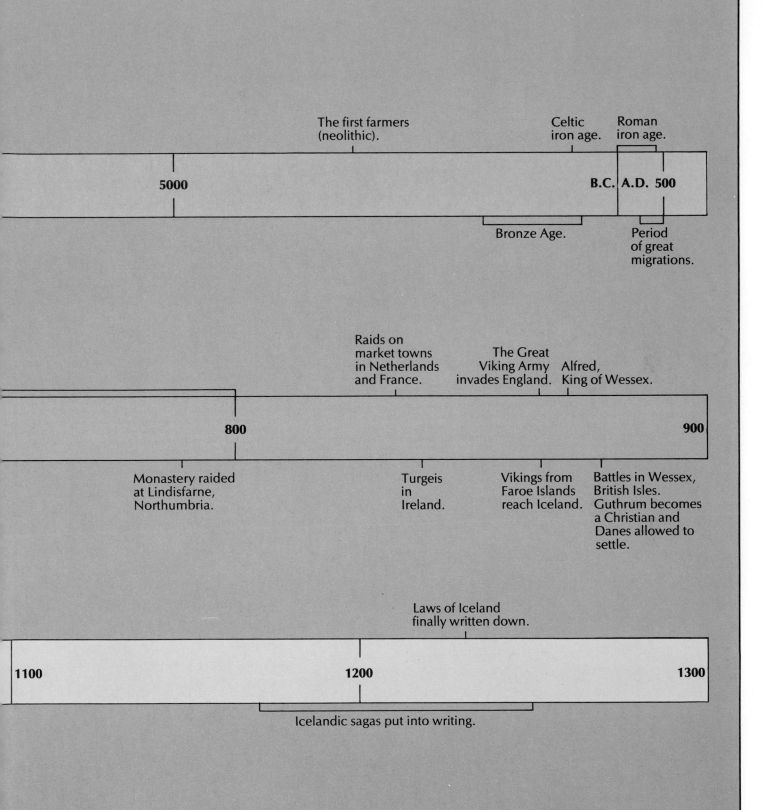

The first farmers (neolithic).

Celtic iron age.

Roman iron age.

5000

B.C. | A.D. 500

Bronze Age.

Period of great migrations.

Raids on market towns in Netherlands and France.

The Great Viking Army invades England.

Alfred, King of Wessex.

800

900

Monastery raided at Lindisfarne, Northumbria.

Turgeis in Ireland.

Vikings from Faroe Islands reach Iceland.

Battles in Wessex, British Isles. Guthrum becomes a Christian and Danes allowed to settle.

Laws of Iceland finally written down.

1100

1200

1300

Icelandic sagas put into writing.

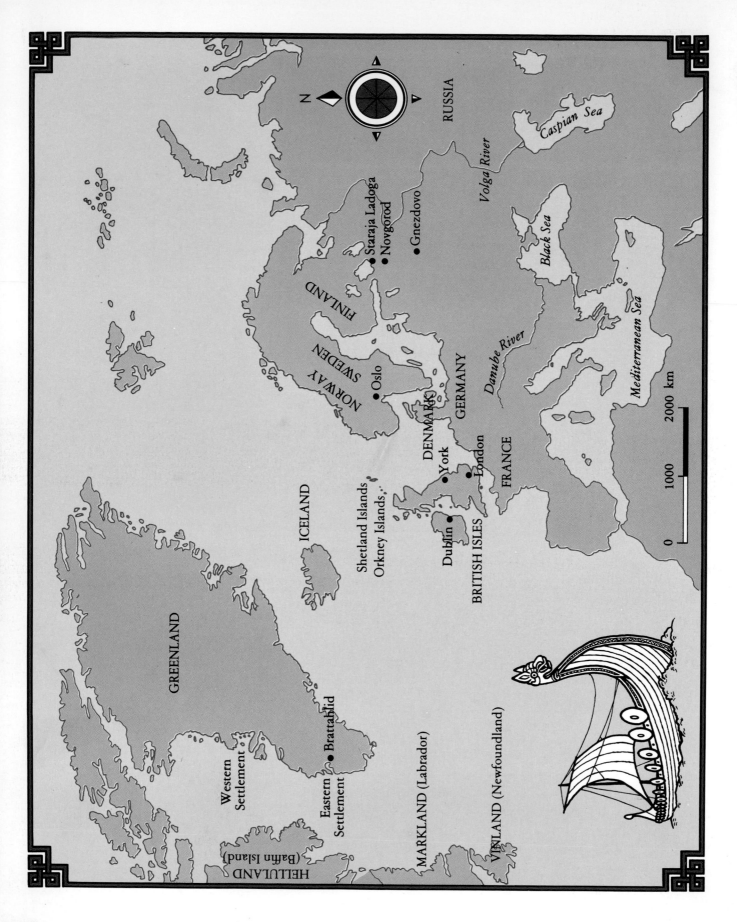

RUSSIA

Caspian Sea

Volga River

Staraja Ladoga
Novgorod
Gnezdovo

Black Sea

FINLAND

SWEDEN

NORWAY

Oslo

Mediterranean Sea

GERMANY

Danube River

DENMARK

York
London

FRANCE

Dublin

BRITISH ISLES

Shetland Islands
Orkney Islands

ICELAND

2000 km

1000

0

GREENLAND

Western
Settlement

Eastern
Settlement

Brattahlid

MARKLAND (Labrador)

VINLAND (Newfoundland)

HELLULAND
(Baffin Island)

The Vikings: Introduction

The Vikings, also called the Norsemen and the Varangians, did not came from any particular country. They came from the cold Scandinavian lands of Denmark, Sweden and Norway. The Germans called them arcomanni or "ship-men", the Arabs in Spain called them el-Majus or "the heathen". The Irish monks called the Norwegians the Finn-gaill or "white foreigners" and the Danes called them the Dubh-gaill or "black foreigners". The two main types of Scandinavians have always been easily recognised: the tall, fair-haired, blue-eyed people and the short, dark-skinned, brown or dark-haired, broad-faced people. They went out from their lands in different directions. Those from Norway went west to the British Isles, Iceland and Greenland. Those from Denmark went south-west to England, France and northern Germany, and those from Sweden went into Finland and Russia.

The Viking Age proper lasted from about A.D. 780 to 1070 and it was during this time that the Vikings moved overseas. They were warriors as well as traders. They travelled widely, both on raids, and in search of trade. The Vikings developed important trade routes, and were the first to journey across the Atlantic to America. They had a great influence on the government and culture of the countries they invaded.

The harsh, cold climate of Scandinavia made the land hard to farm so the Vikings also travelled in search of more land to farm and on which to graze their stock. Like other people they desired the wealth and luxury goods which were available as the trade routes opened and they built fine ships and market towns to make this possible. They used invasion and conquest to gain the things they wanted and also to give power and importance to their rulers and leaders. The Vikings were also great poets and storytellers. Our knowledge of their culture comes from three sources: **archaeology**, **numismatics** (the study of coins and medals) and written records.

Detail from a carved funerary stone showing ship full of Viking warriors, 10th century A.D.

The Viking contribution to European trade eventually made possible the northward expansion of the Christian European civilisation. Christian missionaries began to be sent to Scandinavian countries. They preached against the Viking way of life, particularly disliking the Viking and Muslim slave trade. Eventually some leaders were converted, ordering their people to follow their example, and thus the Viking way of life was dramatically changed.

Also, weak states easily conquered by the earlier Vikings, built up defences, and the Turks, too, began to move into eastern lands and trade routes, and by the 11th century A.D. the Vikings ceased to control any part of England.

The Viking Age ended at the end of the 11th century A.D. There were several reasons for its decline. The three main Scandinavian countries, from which the Vikings came, were not really organised into one fighting force. In fact, they often fought amongst themselves. This made it possible for them to be defeated by other countries. Also these other countries had learnt how to build ships that were as good as the Vikings' and often even better, and they could defeat the Vikings at sea. The gradual conversion of Vikings to Christianity meant that the Viking Age the world had known for 300 years was over.

Broch of Gurness, Orkney: Viking ruins of a wall and interior with well, stairs and partition.

The Importance of Landforms and Climate

The landforms and climate of any area determine to a large extent how people live, what kinds of crops can be grown and where, and what kinds of animals can be kept.

The Scandinavian lands are very mountainous, especially in Norway and Sweden, which means that very little land is available for cultivation and grazing. Only three per cent of the land in Norway could be used for growing crops, only nine per cent of Sweden's land could be farmed, and only half of the land in Denmark, as much of the soil in these countries was very poor.

All of the Scandinavian lands lie in the cold area of the world where in winter there are only a few hours of daylight, and in summer,

The Scandinavian lands are very mountainous leaving little land for growing crops and raising animals.

Sogne Fjord, western Norway – this fjord is 1,234 metres (4,050 feet) deep and is typical of the coastline of the lands once inhabited by the Vikings.

although there are long days, the season is short and still quite cool. For some time each year, large areas are covered with ice and snow. This means that there is only a short time each year when crops can be grown as well as limited land on which to grow them. Having suitable land for grazing, and sufficient shelter was always a problem for farmers keeping animals. People looked to other sources for food such as fishing along the coastline which, in places like Norway, is very rugged with many **fjords**.

The lack of good farmland for the increasing population is thought to be one of the reasons why the Vikings set out to seek new lands. The lands in the warmer climates of Europe and Britain were ideal for farming. Also these lands had commodities which the Scandinavians could not produce in their own countries.

Natural Plants, Animals and Birds

The kinds of plants which grew naturally in the area and the animals and birds that lived among them were also important. With limited farmland the Scandinavians had to learn how to make use of the animals that lived around them.

Most of the area in the cold mountains and **glacial valleys** was covered with dense pine and other forests. Because wood was plentiful it was used for building houses and boats, for firewood, making charcoal and for furniture and utensils.

By studying the behaviour of animals in the wild, Norsemen learnt to trap them for food and fur. Animals such as reindeer, wolverines, lemmings, elk, red deer, bears, lynx and seals were found there.

Birds, including partridges and grouse, found their way to Viking lands on their migration routes and were caught. Eggs of seabirds were also collected and used.

Trout, salmon, cod and herring were among the fish that were regularly caught.

Wolverines inhabited the dense pine forests where the Vikings once lived.

Crops, Herds and Hunting

The Vikings had families and farms to return to at the end of each sea voyage. While they were away their families ran the farms. These people's lives were organised according to the seasons.

In the short growing season the fields were ploughed with horse or ox drawn ploughs and planted with rye, oats, wheat, corn and barley. Like peasant people elsewhere, they performed rituals which they believed would ensure a good harvest. The Scandinavian custom was for the farmer's wife to bake a cake made in the shape of the sun. This was carried with a tankard of ale or mead to the stables where the draught animals were kept. All animals and workmen ate a piece of the cake and the rest was crumbled and put in the seed box to be planted with the seed. Each workman drank from the tankard and the rest of the ale was poured over the animals. In some places in Sweden this custom is still practised.

The Vikings hunted the bull reindeer using bows, arrows and spears.

Vegetables such as cabbages, peas and beans were grown in smaller garden plots. The flax plant was also cultivated.

When Vikings **colonised** their lands in the Hebrides, and Shetland and the Orkney Islands, they carried on these activites in much the same way as they had done in their homelands.

Herds

Cattle, sheep, pigs and poultry were kept for food, wool, hides and feathers. The herd animals were taken to the mountain pastures to graze during the warmer summer months and here families often had small summer farmhouses. Shepherds and sheepdogs watched the sheep. When the cold autumn months began, the animals would be taken down from the mountains (which would soon be snow covered) and housed in animal shelters on the farms. Domesticated cats and dogs were also kept. Dogs were particularly useful as sheep dogs, watch dogs and hunting dogs.

When a farmer was called to sea or to fight there was a ceremonial handing over of the keys of the household to his wife. This symbolised her authority over the house, land, animals and all the household and farm workers. Many of these farms resembled huge estates and the planning and directing of them was a complicated task. The planning and organising of the house routines and dairy had to be done as well.

Hunting and Fishing

Deer, elk, wild boars, bears, rabbits, game birds, and in the more northerly regions, whales, reindeer, polar bears and seals were hunted using spears and bows and arrows. (The very effective Scandinavian bow was later used in Ireland.) Animals were used for other things besides food. Antlers, bones and hides were used for clothing and tents. Hunting was frequently done on horseback. The Vikings were particularly fond of their horses. They cared for them well and often made quite decorative saddles, bridles and spurs. Hunting with falcons was a Viking pastime.

Along the coast, fish were caught with fishing lines and fish traps, and shellfish were collected. Boats were used to go out to catch the deep sea fish.

Iron stirrup with brass inlay dated from late 10th to 11th century. The Vikings also made decorative saddles, bridles and spurs.

Families were important to the Vikings and often the people of a whole village would be related to only a few families. Family loyalty was strong. Ancestors were considered to be part of the living family. Households also had a number of slaves called **thralls**.

Houses

Houses and other buildings were made of wood and had thatched roofs. Some of these could be ten metres (eleven yards) in length with a high pitched roof and were known as long-houses. The one main building, called a **stofa**, was used for eating and sleeping. It had a huge fireplace in the centre and tables and benches were carried in for meals. Benches along the walls were used as beds at night. Walls of the main building were decorated with shields and tapestries. Other farm buildings, called **burs** which sometimes had additional loft sleeping space, were used for sheltering animals, storing grain, hay, equipment and tools. There was also room for a blacksmith and a dairy.

Some houses had sleeping areas with square wooden beds separated from the rest of the house by a thick curtain. Beds had mattresses of straw and were covered with blankets and eiderdowns filled with duck and goose feathers. The Vikings did not have glass windows and probably used the membranes of animals stretched over a frame.

Furniture was often beautifully carved and had many cushions and pillows for comfort.

Reconstruction of a Viking village at York.

Men

Most Norsemen were farmers. It was only when the farm work of ploughing and sowing was finished that the young men went off in the boats "a-viking", which was the way the Scandinavians described this seafaring way of life. Young men from 14 or 15 years of age onwards could go to sea. The head of the farm or village had to ensure that the community and farms operated properly, and that enough food was produced and stored for the winter months. Wood for cooking and for winter fires had to be cut and stored.

Women

Viking women were also involved in the farming. Woman milked the cows and goats and made butter and cheese which was stored in underground cellars. In the autumn many cattle, sheep and goats were slaughtered and the women would salt and store the meat. Fish were also preserved. Foods were pickled in brine and vinegar.

The women also did the spinning, weaving, and dyeing of wool and flax. They sewed, embroidered and made the clothes. Other household tasks including the cleaning, preparation and cooking of daily meals, were done by the women. When the men were away, the women looked after the farm. They would defend the home against attack and also trade with any visiting merchants.

Children

From an early age the children had to assist as part of the community and family in all of these activities. There were no Viking schools. Children were taught skills by other adults. At about 7 to 8 years of age boys were sent away to the house of foster parents. This bound families together that were not related by blood and made sure that boys were given a disciplined upbringing.

Ruins of Viking buildings, Brough of Birsay, Orkney.

Clothes

The Scandinavians were practical people who liked bright colours and ornaments. This is shown by the clothes they wore which were of three types: work and everyday clothes, special occasion clothes, and for the men, battle dress and seagoing clothes. Materials used included home woven wool, fine wool imported from the Netherlands, linen and fur. Silk was obtained by trade with Russian lands. A large length of silk damask interwoven with gold thread was found aboard the *Gokstad* ship. Woven wool, and looms for making braids and laces, were found aboard the *Oseberg* ship. The *Gokstad* and *Oseberg* were Viking ships which are now on display in the Viking Ship Museum in Oslo.

Men's Clothing

Men wore linen undertrousers with thick trousers over the top. (Undertrousers were used also as pyjamas). A long-sleeved shirt made from wool or linen was worn, and over this went a knee length tunic called a **kyrtil**. Kyrtils worn for special occasions were brightly coloured, often scarlet, and trimmed with fur. Men sometimes wore kilts similar to those worn by the Scots. Beards, moustaches and shoulder length hair were worn as protection from the cold.

Opposite: silver plated iron brooch with enamel work and precious stones.

Women's Clothing

Women wore a linen or silk vest under a long-sleeved tunic. A rectangular pinafore reaching to the knee was worn over this. Clothing was held in place by straps and brooches. Chains, held in place with brooches, were often worn and from these hung useful things like keys, scissors and a money purse. A linen apron was also worn for everyday use. Women were also fond of brightly coloured clothes.

Headdresses defined a woman's status. Unmarried and widowed women had long, uncovered hair, and married women tucked their hair beneath a white linen embroidered scarf.

Young girls often wore short skirts.

Both men and women wore heavy cloaks with fur lined hoods called **kapas**. Shoes were leather kneeboots or dress shoes of soft hide sewn with silk and decorated with gold. Both men and women wore hats. Men's hats were either round wool stiffened hats called **skalhatts** or wide brimmed hats for wearing in the fields. Wealthier people could afford Russian hats and a fur lined cloak called a **möttul**, that was fastened with a brooch.

Jewellery

Jewellery was worn as a sign of wealth and for decoration. Silver and gold jewellery were common. Brooches, such as the one shown opposite were used to hold items of clothing in place.

Clothes at Sea

The practical Vikings adapted their clothing to suit their seafaring life. On the cold seas they wore heavy woollen or leather trousers, a sleeveless leather jerkin or a hip length fur lined coat. The clothes they wore over these were made of oiled skin which made them waterproof. Their long hooded cloaks and capes could also be used as blankets.

Sailors often had cloth socks fastened to their trouser legs. They also wore leather boots with fur linings for winter. Gloves and woollen caps kept their hands and heads protected from the cold.

Battle Dress

The Vikings' battle dress was very easy to move in. Battle helmets were made from leather and sometimes covered in iron. Other decorative helmets, some with horns or shaped like birds, were for ceremonies. These would have been uncomfortable and in some cases dangerous for the wearer in battle.

Above: gold jewellery worn by the Vikings including brooches, armlets, necklaces and bracelets.

Right: 10th century leather boot from York. Usually leather boots were lined with fur for the cold winter weather.

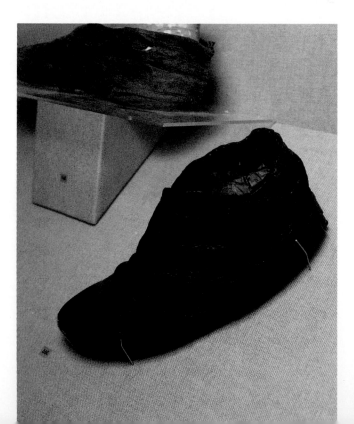

Religion and Rituals of the Vikings

The Vikings believed in many gods. They thought these gods helped their crops to grow and helped them in battle. There were two families of gods called Asar (Aesir) and Vanir.

Important Asar gods

Odin (sometimes called Woden) — chief of gods, god of battle who ruled Asgard, home of the gods. He is depicted as a mysterious one-eyed god.

Tyr — god of war

Balder — Odin's son, god of youth, beauty and goodness

Loki — a troublemaker
(Balder and Loki were not friends.)

Important Vanir gods

Mimir — wisest of the Asar, sent as a hostage to the Vanir but was killed.

Niord — ruler of wind and god of seafaring.

Frey — son of Niord, god of fertility who gave good crops and ensured the survival of the race

Freyja — the daughter who was always attended by cats.

At the great midwinter feast, a boar was always sacrificed to Frey and its head carried in procession.

In addition there were Aegir and his wife Ran who personified the sea, and their nine daughters who were waves of the ocean.

Some places in England and elsewhere still bear names derived from these gods. Our days of the week are also named after them: **Tyr's day**, **Woden's day**, **Thor's day**, and **Frey's day**, to name a few.

The Vikings also believed that each person had a **fylgja** or animal spirit that accompanied them everywhere.

Odin was supposed to have given one of his eyes in return for being able to drink from Mimir's Well of Knowlede beneath Yggdrasil's Ash Tree. Odin also had two ravens named Hugin and Mugin (Thought and Memory). Each day they would fly over the world and return at night to tell Odin all they had seen. Odin at times disguised himself as an old man in a wide brimmed hat and cloak. Adopting the name Grim, he pleaded with the later Christians to return to the old ways of worship.

Yggdrasil's Ash Tree

According to the Vikings, this tree held up the sky and the gods lived beneath it in their home of Asgarth. The long roots of the tree covered Midgarth (the world of mankind), the world of the Frost Giants, and the world of the dead, called Hel.

At the root of the tree was the Well of Knowledge and the Well of Fate. At the Well of Fate lived three Norns — Past, Present and Future who wove a huge cloth in which every thread represented the life of a person. When someone died their thread in the cloth was cut.

The Vikings made sacrifices to the gods, especially during the three main festivals:

Vetrarblot — mid-October, when sacrifices were made to ensure a good winter.
Jolablot or **Midsvetrarblot** — mid-Janunary when sacrifices were made to ensure good crops. Sacrifices were always made to Frey.
Sigrblot — in April when sacrifices were made for victories at war.

At these festivals people ate horsemeat and drank bowls of wine. Sometimes animals given to the gods were not killed, but were dedicated to the god and the owner could still use the animal.

After Death

The Vikings believed that after death the spirits of the good were rewarded and the spirits of the bad were punished. The spirit was supposed to sail to a new life. Many important people were buried at sea or in ships with their possessions. Those who were buried on land had stones placed around their grave in the shape of a ship. In Iceland, graves with boats or ships are rare. Here the main way to travel was by horse and over two thirds of Icelandic graves have the remains of one or more horses buried with the person.

Brave warriors were supposed to go to Valhalla, (Odin's paradise) to celebrate and await Ragnarök, (the end of the world).

Ragnarök — the End of the World

This would be the time when the gods would be killed by giants and monsters. The sign that this was about to happen would be three years of winter and three years of war. Huge wolves would then swallow the sun and the moon and the enormous serpent called Midgarthsorm who was coiled around the earth would rise up from the sea.

The watchman, Bifrost, who sat on the rainbow bridge leading to the land of Asgarth, would watch for the Giants to come. When they appeared, his job was to summon the warriors from Valhalla even though it was known that they too would be overpowered. The wolf Fenrir would eat Odin; Thor would be poisoned by the serpent which would also die; the Fire Giant, Surt would kill Frey. The stars would then fall from the sky and the earth would sink into the sea. But, it was believed, some would survive, and those survivors would build a new and better world that would rise up out of the sea.

Opposite: woven tapestry which shows the Norse gods Odin, Thor and Frey. Odin carries his axe, Thor his hammer, and Frey an ear of corn. Odin's name was bestowed on very few places but he is well remembered in literature and was regarded as the god of poetry. He was also god of wisdom. Thor was a god common to all early Germanic peoples and was sometimes regarded as secondary to Odin and in some traditions as Odin's son. Place names in England suggest that Thor (or Thunor as he was called in English) was well known in Saxon and Jutish areas. Frey had other names as well, Yngi or Yngvi-Freyr and was the imaginary father of north Germanic tribes. He was worshipped especially in Sweden as well as being well known in Norway and Iceland.

Temples

The Vikings built temples to their gods and descriptions of them can be found in the sagas and the writings of the early Christians. There was one famous central temple built and maintained by the Swedish kings at Uppsala where the great Viking celebration was held every ninth year. The temple stood beside three great burial mounds of the kings. After it was destroyed, the Christians built a church over it. Even today people can go through the trap door of this church into the foundations of the old pagan Viking temple. This temple was still being used in A.D. 1070 and was the chief centre of resistance to the new religion of Christianity.

Ruins of a Viking boat burial — the stones are placed around the grave in the shape of a boat. Important people were buried in their boats at sea or on land.

The Coming of Christianity

Missionaries were sent from England and Germany to convert the Vikings to Christianity, but they were often thrown out of the Viking lands. Often they left of their own accord as they were not able to convert the Vikings.

Eventually, some of the Viking kings saw that being a Christian would give them advantages when dealing with other Christian rulers in Europe. In about A.D. 960 Harald Bluetooth, King of Denmark, became a Christian and decreed that all his subjects were also to become Christians.

The Norwegians rejected Christianity and also rejected their new king, Haakon the Good,

because he became a Christian. Their new king, Olaf Tryggvason, became a Christian and he threatened to put to death anyone who refused to be converted. He also held visiting Icelanders hostage until the people there accepted the new religion. The Icelanders eventually accepted Christianity but also continued to practise their old religions in secret. This was the decision of the **Althing**, their parliament and place of law.

The people of Sweden resisted the Christians until A.D. 1008 when their king became a Christian. Their traditional temple still remained until the 12th century.

Obeying the Law

"With law shall the land be built up and with lawlessness wasted away". This is what the Vikings said and believed.

Viking law involved all free people (**karls**). Thralls or slaves had few rights under the law but it seems that they were not treated badly by the families who owned them. Free people, including the chief person of a village or town, (**jarls**), formed parliaments called **Things**, where all law was preserved, decided, judged and spoken. The Things grew up around the communities they served. The head of every family had to go to the Thing, and women went in place of their husbands if they were away. People also came to listen. Before the coming of Christianity the Things chose the kings, and the kings were considered holy.

Viking law was not written down but memorised by individuals and spoken aloud. Frequently a community would choose a young man to learn the law for two or three years. On his return he would then be their legal adviser.

The Vikings had many laws. There were laws regarding boundaries of properties, hunting rights, felling of trees, making of love songs, turning people's butter sour, offences against people, hurting the community, marriage, divorce and inheritance, religious observance and fair fighting. The law was concerned with the dignity and value of the individual in the society and punishment was ordered accordingly.

Punishments and Settlements

In many cases the law was quite clear and punishments were decided in an agreed way. In other cases offences were sometimes settled by duelling, with set rules for declaring winners and losers. Another way of settling disputes was to put an individual through a painful ordeal, such as having to grasp hot metal. They would judge whether the person was guilty or innocent depending on how the wound healed.

On the whole the Vikings were obedient to the laws, accepting the judgement of the Thing, and they found it helped them to live in a stable, honest and reasonably safe community.

The oldest parliament in the world, the **Althing of Iceland**, was established in A.D. 930. It met each year and thousands of people went to listen to the lawspeakers. At the annual meeting of the Althing people also had a chance to exchange information about trade and events as well as engage in entertainment and story-telling. It was by the decision of the Althing in A.D. 1000 that Christianity was accepted in Iceland as the official religion although people were still allowed to practise their old religion. The laws of Iceland were finally written down in about A.D. 1230 after the Viking Age was over.

Danelaw

Danelaw referred to that part of England in which Danish, not English law was followed. It included the Danish conquered lands in Northumbria, East Anglia, the Five Boroughs of Stamford, Leicester, Derby, Nottingham and Lincoln, and the south-west midlands. The southern boundary was established by the treaty made in A.D. 886 between King Alfred and Guthram of East Anglia.

Writing it Down: Recording Things

The way in which the Scandinavians recorded most things was to remember them. Their **sagas** and long poems were not written down until the Middle Ages after Christian monks had taught some people to write in Latin on parchment.

The Vikings did have an alphabet, called a **runic alphabet**, which started just before or at the beginning of the Christian era. It first had 24 letters (or phonetic symbols) but this was changed by A.D. 700 to 16 letters. It was known as the **futhark**, from its first letters, just as our alphabet is called the ABC. Only some Vikings could read and write in runes.

Runes carved into stone, found on Orkney Islands.

28

It is not known exactly where or how this runic alphabet began but there are traces of Latin, Greek, Etruscan and other languages in it. Viking legend says that the alphabet was a gift from the god Odin. Because the writing was mainly vertical and diagonal strokes with no curves, it is thought to have been originally intended to be carved on wood and stone. There was also a magical meaning in runes which were used in a special way for spells and magic. Runes carved in small sticks were supposed to be for blessings, spells and curses. Runic inscriptions have been found from Greenland to the Black Sea, and from the Isle of Man to Athens, although few have been found in Iceland. About 500 have been found in Denmark, about 750 in Norway and about 3,000 in Sweden.

Vikings carved their runes in long ribbons which covered the surface of a stone. They were painted in bright colours and set beside a public roadway for all to read.

Rune stones, showing the runic alphabet used by the Vikings.

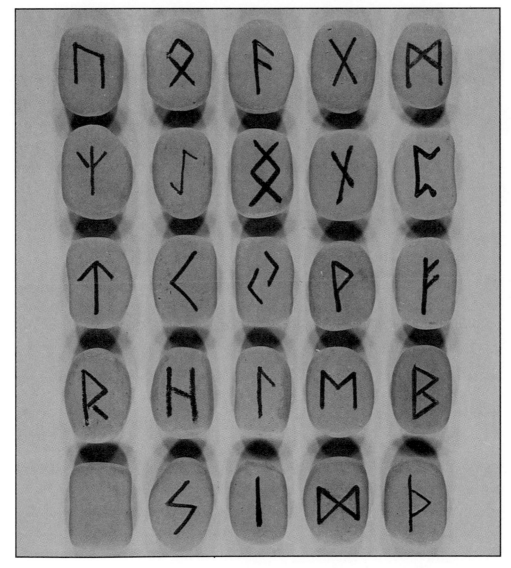

Viking Legends and Literature

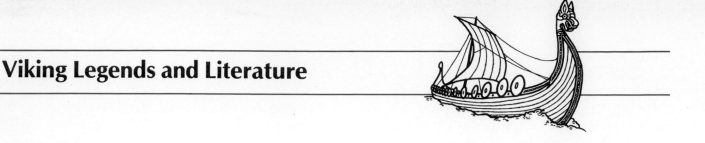

The sagas the Vikings told were a mixture of fact and myth, designed mainly to entertain. Two of the best known sagas, the Saga of Burnt Njal and the Laxdale Saga, have been translated into English. The most important sagas are about the Viking discovery of America.

They are the Sagas of the Norse Kings, collected and written down by an Icelander called Snorri Sturluson. The sagas, legends and stories the Vikings told were passed on by word of mouth from one generation to another. They were not written down until long after the Viking Age ended.

The Vikings took great pleasure in listening to the **skalds**, who were the poets and the storytellers.

Some Legendary Sagas

Name	What it is about
Njal's saga	Greatest of the sagas. About the characters of many people who come into contact with a farmer and his sage as they try to combat evil forces in society.
Edda	About the old gods of the north including a tragic tale of Balder and a comic tale of Thor's journey into Giantland.
Fridthjófs saga	A romantic love story.
Grettis saga	About a hero who fights against heavy odds but who is finally slain.
Hœnsa-thoris saga	About a poor man who becomes rich as a pedlar and decides to become a landowner but is unpopular.
Bandamanna saga	About chiefs who come to no good by trying to profit from other people's mistakes.
Eyrbyggja saga	About a feuding family.
	These are just a few. There are many others.

Histories

Icelandic historians and others began writing about the end of the 11th century when the Viking Age proper was over. Saemundr Sigfússon, who learned Latin as a priest in France, wrote a Latin history of the kings of Norway but this has since been lost. However, Ari Thorgilsson's Islendingabók (Book of the Icelanders) has survived which covers c A.D.118 to 870. Landnámabók (Book of Settlement) is another that has survived. Others were also written.

Drapas

Drapas were special poems composed in praise of the king and written by poets who lived in the king's court. They were well rewarded for their efforts.

Above: detail of carved portal of Hyllestad Stave-church. Setesdal — scene from the story of Sigurd, where he kills the dragon. Such legends represented Viking ideals of courage, bravery, ruthlessness and cunning.

Right: Thor hammer pendant.

Art and Architecture

The Vikings acquired many beautiful objects by way of trade but they also produced art of their own. They made beautiful gold and silver ornaments by melting down gold and silver which they got through trade. They were excellent metal craftsmen and produced ornaments and beautifully crafted and decorated weapons. Animals were a favourite subject of Scandinavian artists.

Carved head post from the Oseberg ship.

Wood Carving

The Vikings were excellent wood carvers. Wood was plentiful and many everyday things were made from it including dishes, troughs, casks, buckets, and furniture. Most of their furniture had intricately carved designs. The contents of the Gokstad and Oseberg ships are examples of the Viking wood carver's art. The ship's prow, the waggons, three sledges and other items on board were made by artists of the early ninth century. Some of the carvings on these items tell a story.

Picture Stones

In Gotland there are hundreds of memorial stones which were produced from the fifth century onwards. These show many things such as ships going on voyages, men fighting in battle, and warriors being welcomed to Valhalla. These are the art galleries of the Viking Age.

Architecture

No examples of kings' halls, temples, hill forts or farm buildings have survived as these were built of wood and easily destroyed. But archaeological evidence shows that the Vikings erected their buildings with good proportions, solid workmanship and high artistic finish which would have matched that of their Viking ships.

Ship Building

Perhaps the works which best show both the Viking artisty and superb engineering design are the Viking ships themselves. In recent years several of these ships have been discovered and studied by archaeologists. Two of the most famous are the Oseberg ship and the Gokstad ship, which had been buried for over 1,000 years. The 21 metre (68 feet) Oseberg ship is thought to have been a pleasure craft for sheltered waters because of its shallow draft, but the 24 metre (79 feet) long Gokstad ship may have been a raiding vessel.

Gokstad Ship

The Gokstad ship was made of wide oak planks with a stepped mast. It had a double ended bow that swept gracefully to a high stem or stern. The ship has no carvings but is superbly designed for speed.

Oseberg Ship

Apart from the beauty of its design, the Oseberg ship was superbly carved from stem to stern. The carvings are mostly of animals. One historian worte:

> "No-one who has ever looked at the Oseberg ship can ever again think of the ninth century Norsemen as completey vile and soulless barbarians."

Detail of wooden carving showing the Saga of Sigurd Favnesbane. After the forging of the sword Gram, it is tested and breaks.

Many of the Viking ships were beautifully carved from stem to stern.

33

Going Places: Transport, Exploration and Communication

The shortage of good farmland in Scandinavia and the desire for wealth and possessions which could be traded or seized in other lands, prompted the Vikings to venture out from their homelands. They learned to build fine ships to enable them to do this. The map below shows the extent of the Vikings' travels.

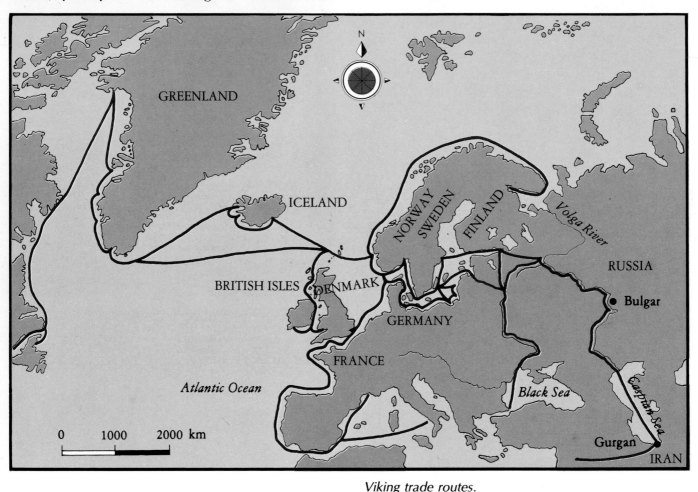

Viking trade routes.

Their wide beamed trading ships called **knörr** brought to the north gold, silver, ceramics, glassware, fine fabrics, jewels, and wine. These had been traded for bearskins and other furs, walrus ivory, reindeer hides and antlers, amber, wax and slaves. Traders also made their way down navigable rivers in small boats but they had to make sure that they returned before the northern rivers froze in winter. They travelled down the Volga to Bulgar where they built a temporary trading village of wooden huts, paying one tenth of their slaves for this privilege. From here they were able to send out trading parties who finally reached Gurgan in Iran.

Other items exchanged in Viking trade were horses, honey, malt, wheat, whale-oil, butter, spices, arrows, fish teeth and fish-lime, hawks, coins, hazelnuts, cattle, swords and soap-stone pots, axe-heads, silks, millstones and coins. However, it is difficult to know how much of the wealth brought home was obtained by way of trade and how much by plunder, piracy and looting. Trade was peaceful but we know that the Vikings were not always peaceful.

Viking scales — equipment of a merchant

Detail from carved funerary stone from Gotland shows a Viking ship with a chequered mast.

Raiding and Plundering

We know from the accounts of the monks in the monasteries in France, England and elsewhere, and from the sagas that the Vikings landed, raided, destroyed and looted along the coastlines.

Colonisation

We do not know a great deal about the earliest Norse settlements from A.D. 780 onwards but these appear to have been peaceful and not concerned with plundering and looting. They were made by Vikings in search of new farm and pasture land where they could establish a home and carry on with the same kind of farming life that they were used to in Scandinavia. The main areas where colonies were founded were explored and taken over after A.D. 860.

In England, the Danes conquered much of the north-east and took and bought land from the English. Here they established peaceful settlements or colonies. They settled elsewhere in Europe, such as in Normandy in France, and Staraja Ladoga in Finland in the same way.

The urge to explore sent the Vikings out to eventually discover Iceland and Greenland where they established settlements. Thousands of emigrants left Scandinavian homes, packed their belongings and animals into a boat and set off. Entire families were quite prepared to face any danger and settle in new and strange lands. Some of these voyages in open boats lasted seven days or longer.

The Vikings had discovered North America long before Christopher Columbus. The Icelander Bjarni Herjolfsson in A.D. 986 was the first European to see North America and Leif Eriksson in Bjarni's ship later went to see for himself.

To enable them to reach their destinations and ensure a safe return, the Vikings were masters of sea-lore. They learned the meanings of different cloud formations, the colour of water which might indicate shallows or rivers flowing into the sea from nearby land, the closeness of land by the numbers and kind of sea creatures, birds, driftwood, seaweed and the feel of the wind. They invented several primitive **navigational devices** such as the **sun board**, the **shadow board** and the **sunstone**. They did not have maps or magnetic compasses.

Music, Dancing and Recreation

Entertaining each other at feasts was a favourite social pastime of the Scandinavians, especially during the long winter months. Such feasts were very elaborate with the best food and drink being offered, and people would wear their most beautiful clothes and jewels. Skalds, the visiting storytellers, would entertain people with stories, poems and ballads sometimes accompanied by music. The simplest musical instruments used in folk music were rattles, flutes, whistles, harps, long wooden trumpets and fiddles. We know very little about the songs of the Vikings, for like everything else in Viking culture, these would have been taught by word of mouth. Neither are details of dances known. Vikings did sing and dance, especially at festivals, so the writings of the missionaries tell us. The missionaries did not approve of the Viking pagan dances and discouraged and forbade them.

Games

The Vikings had board games similar to draughts and chess. Outdoor games included ball games and fencing. A games cabinet, designed to be used as a draughtsboard, and draughtsmen were found on the Gokstad ship.

Hunting was a recreational activity as well as a way of obtaining food supplies. Hunting and racing hawks were also kept as well as magnificent white hunting falcons.

Skiing

On land the people of the north were expert at travelling over ice and snow, usually to hunt. It is known that the Vikings were using skis in the 10th and 11th centuries and Norse myths mention Ull (sometimes Skade), the ski god and Undurridis, the ski goddess. The oldest skis in the world have been found in the bogs of Sweden and Finland and are believed to be 4,000 to 5,000 years old. Cave paintings dating from 2000 B.C. in Norway also show people on skis.

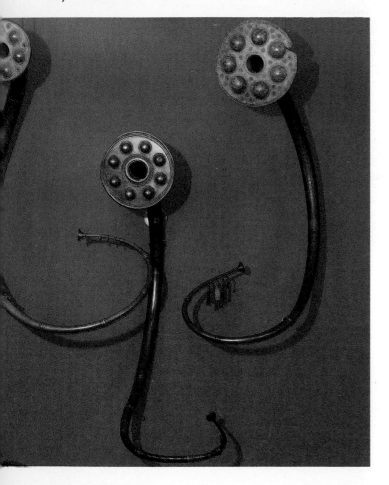

These late Bronze Age trumpets, called Lurs, were discovered in a peat bog in Denmark. Little is known about how they are played or the music played upon them.

36

Wars and Battles

Battles including family feuds, raids, and fights in defence of property were constantly being waged by the Vikings. There was no permanent army. Every male from fifteen years of age was taught to fight and each accepted without question that he should do so. When a lord (or jarl) wished to raise an army or a raiding party, he would send out war arrows. When a farming community or village was summoned in this way, the eligible men would depart at once with their weapons of axes, spears, swords, bows and arrows. Men from a community would form a fighting unit because they could recognise each other by sight. Some fighting units could be as small as 60 men or as large as 400. After a battle or raid, those who had fought would receive a share of the plunder or gifts from the jarl.

Detail from Gundestrup cauldron — thought to be a Celtic work brought to Denmark by the Vikings as plunder.

Swords

These were prized possessions which might have been handed down from father to son. Many stories were told about swords including tales of magic swords and swords which were gifts from the gods. Some had magic charms or **runes** engraved on them. A sign of peace was for a man to tie his sword in its scabbard with a strap because it meant he could not draw the sword quickly.

Shields

Each man in battle carried a wooden or metal shield. There were also special white shields that would be held up during battle to show that the Vikings were ready to discuss terms of peace. If this was declined, the battle would continue.

Some Well Known Viking Invasions and Battles

When	Where	What Happened
A.D. 789	Lindisfarne, Northumbria, British Isles	A monastery was raided, sacked and looted
A.D. 834	Netherlands & France	Raids on market towns
A.D. 850–860	Ireland	Norwegians already living in the Hebrides invaded Ireland and settled there. The Danes also invaded Ireland.
A.D. 876	York (British Isles)	Norwegians invaded and settled in Northumbria.
A.D. 878	Battles in Wessex (British Isles)	Alfred the Great finally defeated the Danish leader Guthrum after many battles. The Danes were allowed to settle provided Guthrum became a Christian.
A.D. 911	Normandy (France)	After battles and invasions, the Viking chief, Rollo, was allowed to settle. Many Vikings eventually married Christian Frankish women. Rollo became a Christian.
A.D. 1030	Battle of Stiklaestad (Svold near Vinland)	King Olaf of Norway killed.
A.D. 1066	Battle of Stamford Bridge (England)	King Harald Hardrada, king of Norway killed by King Harold of England.
A.D. 1066	Battle of Hastings (England)	The Normans were descendants of the Vikings. Norman Duke William invaded England and defeated the Saxon King, Harold, thereby becoming King William I of England

Many of these battles are recounted in the sagas and histories.

Viking Inventions and Special Skills

Shipbuilding

It was in the seventh century that the Vikings perfected the building and sailing of their ships. The design was unique to the Vikings who combined superb craftsmanship, design and efficiency. They had a keel which was designed to sail a set course, a sturdy mast and a single full sail which propelled the ship at great speeds before the wind. The sails were of woven coarse wool and dyed bright colours. The sides of the ships were high to keep the sailors dry and were often gilded and ornamented so as to display the owner's wealth and power. Oars were used when the sail was not appropriate. Ships for long distance trade and colonisation were of slightly different design.

Coins

Vikings introduced their own coins to the areas where they settled. Coins made trading much easier than the old system of barter which means exchanging goods for goods. The record of coins struck by various rulers also helps historians to better understand when events happened and the symbols on coins tell us what was important at that time.

Byzantine and Islamic coins — part of Viking treasures found in burials. The Vikings fashioned their own coins.

Navigational Instruments

Apart from using the North Star at night, the Vikings invented three devices to help them to navigate their ships. These were the sunboard, sunstone and shadow board.

Sunboard

This had a dial in the centre on which were marked the points of the compass. The Vikings took a bearing from the rising or setting sun. Sources also say that the Vikings took readings at noon as well.

Sunstone

This was a crystal of **cordierite** (also used in jewellery) which changes colour from yellow to dark blue when held at right angles to polarised light from the sun, whether the sun is visible or not. This stone would change colour on overcast days and even when the sun was 7° below the horizon.

Shadow board

This looked like a sundial with a board on which concentric circles (circles having the some centre) were drawn, and an adjustable centre stick. The height of the centre stick would be set so at noon the shadow would fall on a particular circle. By keeping the shadow on the same circle each noon the ship would maintain the same course.

Democratic Justice

The Viking Thing, which was their parliament, law court and meeting place, was one of the first in the world. It allowed individuals to have some say in the making of laws. The Thing also served the community as a whole and not just the interests of a few. Everyone was given equal rights before the law. The Vikings were also the first people to use a jury of 12 ordinary people to judge if someone was guilty or not guilty.

Parliament Plains where the National Assembly, the Althing, met.

40

Why the Civilisation Declined

By the middle of the 11th century the Viking Age was over. The weak states the Vikings had easily conquered three centuries earlier had become more prepared. They had raised powerful armies to resist invaders and to drive the Vikings out. They were driven out of England.

The trade route to the east through Russia began to be less popular as the Mediterranean route was re-opened after the First Crusade. The good relations between Sweden and Russia also came to an end.

The Vikings came into contact with Christians who had made their way to the Scandinavian lands and this changed their culture. Some of the Viking kings became Christians and in turn decreed that all their subjects were to become Christians. Some became Christians because they thought that they might have an advantage when dealing with other Christian leaders in Europe. Many Vikings, especially the Norwegians and Swedes, resisted Christianity with its new beliefs and teachings and repeatedly expelled the missionaries who tried to convert them. Some people such as the Icelanders practised both religions. They did not want to become Christian, but because they were at the mercy of the Christian king Olaf who controlled their trade, they agreed. Christianity by its constant preaching, especially against the slave trade and other aspects of the Viking culture, gradually undermined this culture.

The Vikings too had changed. The people who went out to establish colonies elsewhere adapted to their new environment, often intermarrying with the people of those lands and adopting their ways.

The Vikings were not conquered and they did not disappear. They changed as the world changed but the legacy of the Viking Age is still with us.

Descendants of the Vikings still exist today; they changed as the world changed around them.

Glossary

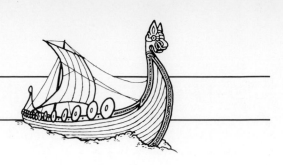

Althing The parliament in Iceland established in A.D. 930. It met beside the Oxara River every year. Its advisers formed a legislature called logretta. Lawspeakers would announce the laws of Iceland from the "Hill of Laws".

Archaeology The study of a culture by carefully digging up, describing and studying the remains of that culture.

Beriberi A painful disease which causes the body to swell up. It is caused by not having enough vitamin B1 in the diet.

Bur A farm building additional to the main building, used for storing equipment or sheltering animals.

Charcoal A product made by burning wood very slowly. Charcoal contains carbon which blacksmiths used to work iron.

Colonise Establish a settlement in another country or area.

Cordierite A mineral found in Scandinavia. When held at right angles to rays of polarised light from the sun, it changes colour from yellow to dark blue.

Democratic When power or authority is given to the people who use it on their own behalf. This is very different to a government where people are told what to do and are unable to make suggestions or change that direction.

Drapas Poems composed in praise of a king by a poet who usually lived in the king's court. It usually praised the king's courage and skill in battle and his generosity toward his people.

Eld-Hus Name given to a kitchen or cooking house which was separate from the main building or house.

Fjord A long narrow arm of sea bordered by steep cliffs. Many fjords exist along the coast of Norway.

Flail A tool for threshing grain by hand. It consists of a handle with a freely swinging stick or bar attached to the end of it.

Flas A plant with blue flowers. The fibres from the stems were used to make linen (cloth).

Futhark The name given to the runic alphabet from its first letters, in the same way as our alphabet is called the ABC.

Fylgja Animal spirit that was believed to accompany all Vikings.

Gilded Covered with gold or of a gold colour.

Glacial Valley A valley which has or has had large masses of ice and snow. The ice cuts away the earth as it moves down the valley to the sea. When glaciers melt they leave behind sharp steep valleys.

Heathen A person who is not a Christian.

Jarl A wealthy chief or landowner.

Kapa A long heavy cloak with a fur hood.

Karl A free person. This included all Scandinavians who were not thralls (slaves).

Knörr A wide beamed Viking trading ship.

Kyrtil A knee length tunic worn by men. Kyrtils worn for special occasions were often dyed scarlet and trimmed with fur.

Möttul A fur lined mantle or cloak worn by the wealthy.

Navigational Aiding in navigating or setting and plotting the course of ships.

Numismatics A study of coins and medals.

Rapids Part of a river where the water flows very quickly over a steep slope or rocks. Navigating a boat through rapids is very dangerous.

Runes Letters used to make up the runic alphabet used by the Scandinavians.

Runic Alphabet An alphabet used by the Vikings usually for carving inscriptions on wood or stone. It originally had 24 letters but later had 16.

Saga A Scandinavian story told by storytellers (skalds) to entertain. Sagas usually told of achievements and events in history or of a family or person. They were part truth and part myth, or completely myth.

Scurvy A disease which makes the gums bleed and swell and spots appear on the skin. It is caused by lack of vitamin C in the diet.

Shadow Board A Viking instrument to assist in navigating ships.

Skald A Viking poet or storyteller who travelled from place to place entertaining people. They composed poems and stories as well as telling well-known tales.

Skalhatts Round stiff wool hats worn by men.

Skali Name given to a kitchen or cook house which was separate from the main house or building.

Skyr A dairy food made from creamy curds.

Stofa The main building in a Viking settlement. This building was used for eating and sleeping.

Sunboard A Viking instrument used to assist in navigating ships.

Sunstone A Viking instrument used to assist in navigating ships.

Thing A type of Viking parliament and law court which served the immediate area and was composed of chiefs or jarls in that area.

Thrall A slave. Vikings were slave traders.

The Vikings: Some Famous People and Places

ERIK THE RED

Erik Thorvaldson, who in his youth was nicknamed Erik the Red, was founder of the first European settlement in Greenland and was father of Leif Eriksson. Erik the Red was exiled from Iceland in about A.D. 980 and set out to explore the land to the west, Greenland, which was visible from the mountain tops of Iceland. He sailed to Greenland with his family and livestock, spent his exile there exploring, and returned to Iceland in 986.

A return expedition of 25 ships was organised but only 14 ships and 350 colonists are believed to have landed safely. About 1,000 Scandinavians lived in the colony by 1000 but many died of an epidemic in 1002. The rest of the population gradually died out.

LEIF ERIKSSON

Leif Eriksson was a Norse explorer who is thought to have been the first European to reach America. He was a member of an early Viking voyage to America. He purchased Bjarni Herjolfsson's ship and obtained as much information as possible from him and set out in 1001 with a crew of 35. He reached landfall (thought to have been Baffin Island) and named it Helluland. He made his second landfall near Cape Porcupine. The third landfall was at Newfoundland.

He was the second son of Erik the Red and nicknamed Leif the Lucky. Leif was converted to Christianity by Olaf I Tryggvason and sent by him to convert the people of Greenland.

BJARNI HERJOLFSSON

Bjarni Herjolfsson was an Icelander who first sighted Vinland and who made Leif Eriksson aware of its existence. It is thought that he sighted America while being blown off course on his way to Greenland, which he finally reached. Bjarni Herjolfsson did not go ashore on the new land he had sighted. This was later to be Leif Eriksson's privilege.

KING OLAF TRYGGVASON

King Olaf was a Viking king of Norway who forced his people to accept Christianity. Olaf was supposed to have fled with his mother Astrid to the court of St Fladimir of Russia when his father Tryggvi Olafsson was killed by Harald Graycloak.

In 991 he was a party in the Viking attacks on England and succeeded King Haakon the Great as King of Norway in 995. He had been confirmed in his Christianity in 994. He succeeded in imposing Christianity on his people in some areas. He was killed in the Battle of Svolder about 1000.

REYKJAVIK

This is the largest town and capital of Iceland. It was founded in 874 by Ingólfur Arnarson. Its name means "Bay of Smokes" because of the effects of nearby geysers, steaming springs and boiling mud holes.

FLOKI VILGERDARSON

Floki was a Norwegian and, like Naddod and a Swede named Gardar Svavarson, he was an explorer and *Vikingr Mikill*, "Viking of note". He set out to find the newly discovered island called Gardarsholm. He sailed from south-west Norway, landing first at the Shetlands and then to the Faroes and finally to Iceland which he named. It was to here the Vikings sailed, not as conquerors, but as settlers.

SNORRI STURLUSON

Snorri Sturluson was an Icelandic poet, historian and chieftain and was the author of the *Prose Edda* and also thought to have been the author of *Egils Saga*. He married an heiress and lived at Reykjaholt (Reykholt) where he wrote most of his works. From 1220 to 32 he was the "law speaker" of the Icelandic high court.

He explains in the *Prose Edda* about the skalds and their poetry. He retold the old Norse myths in his works. He also wrote the life story of Olaf of Norway and included in this, a history of Norwegian kings from the time of their legendary descent from Odin.

HARALD I FAIRHAIR

Harald Fairhair was a Scandinavian warrior-chief and the first king to claim sovereignty of all of Norway. He succeeded his father, Halvdan the Black at the age of ten. As a warrior he succeeded in controlling many districts. Many of his subjects emigrated to England when forced to endure Harald's system of taxation.

An account of his life was written down in later years by Snorri Sturluson in his *Heimskringla*.

HARALD HARDRAADE

He was King of Norway from 1045 to 1066. He died in the Battle of Samford Bridge, Yorkshire, England against the forces of the English king Harold II.

Harald Hardraade fought at the age of fifteen against the Danes with King Olaf at the Battle of Stiklestad in 1030 where Olaf was killed. He then fled to Russia but returned in 1045 to rule Norway with his nephew Magnus I Olafsson. Magnus died in battle against Denmark. Harald expanded the Viking lands to include Orkney, Shetland and the islands of the Hebrides. In 1066 he attempted to conquer England but in spite of early successes in battles, his troops were defeated and he was killed.

ISLEIFR

Isleifr, who lived from about 1005 to 1080 was one of the first Icelandic scholars who gained his education after the introduction of the Latin alphabet to Iceland. He was first educated and ordained as a priest and later consecrated as a bishop. His school at Skalhot in Iceland remained a main centre of learning for many centuries.

ARI THORGILSSON

Ari Thorgilsson who lived from about 1067 to 1148 is regarded as Iceland's "father of history". He is credited with having written the history *Islendingabók*, *The Book of the Icelanders* and the *Landnamabok*, *The Book of Settlements*. There are a few other historical works from this period but their authors are not known. Ari was not the first historian. The earliest remembered historian was Saemundr the Wise who lived from 1056 to 1133.

Index

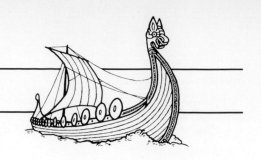

Acknowledgements

The author and publishers are grateful to the following for permission to reproduce copyright photographs and prints:

ANT/NHPA pp. 13, 14; Coo-ee Picture Library p. 11; Ron Sheridan's Photo-Library pp. 9, 10, 15, 16, 17, 27 right, 26, 28; Stock Photos p. 41; Universitetets Oldsaksamling pp. 18, 32; Werner Forman Archive pp. 12, 20, 27 left, 24, 31, 33, 34, 36, 39, 40 and the cover photograph.

While every care has been taken to trace and acknowledge copyright, the publishers tender their apologies for any accidental infringement where copyright has proved untraceable. They would be pleased to come to a suitable arrangement with the rightful owner in each case.

Copyright © Pamela Odijk 1989

No paragraph of this publication may be reproduced, copied or transmitted save with written permission or in accordance with the provisions of the Copyright Act 1956 (as amended), or under the terms of any licence permitting limited copying issued by the Copyright Licensing Agency, 33–4 Alfred Place, London WC1E 7DP.

Any person who does any unauthorised act in relation to this publication may be liable to criminal prosecution and civil claims for damages.

First published in Australia by
THE MACMILLAN COMPANY OF AUSTRALIA PTY LTD
107 Moray Street, South Melbourne 3205
6 Clarke Street, Crows Nest 2065

Published simultaneously in Great Britain in 1989 by
Macmillan Publishers Limited,
4 Little Essex Street, London, WC2R 3LF.

Associated companies and representatives
throughout the world

British Library Cataloguing in Publication Data

Odijk, Pamela
  The Vikings.
  1. Vikings, Social life,
  I. Title II. Series
  948'.02

  ISBN 0–333–49268–4

Set in Optima by Setrite Typesetters, Hong Kong
Printed in Hong Kong

Oceania | Europe | Africa

c50 000 B.C. Aborigines inhabit continent

40 000 Evolution of man

Time	Australian Aborigines	Maori	Melanesians	Greeks	Romans	Angles, Saxons & Jutes	Britons	Vikings	Egyptians	First Africans
8000 B.C.	Torres and Bass Straits under water							The Baltic — freshwater lake		Farm settlements
7500										
7000	Lake Nitchie settled			Neolithic Age						
6500				Settled agriculture						
6000										
5500										
5000	South Australian settlements								Egypt-early farms	Increased trade across Sahara
4500										
4000							Hunting and gathering			
3500	Ord Valley settlement								Predynastic	
3000				Bronze Age				The first farmers		
2500				Crete — palaces					Old Kingdom / Giza pyramids	
2000				Mainland building			Megalithic monuments raised		Middle Kingdom	Sahara becomes desert
1500								Bronze Age	New Kingdom	
1000				Dark Age			Farms and buildings established		New Kingdom declines	Kushites
500 B.C.				Colonisation / City-states established / Classical Age / Wars — lands extended	Rome found / Republic established / Rome expands through Italy and foreign lands		Ogham alphabet in use	Celtic Iron Age / Roman Iron Age	Persian conquest / Greek conquest / Roman rule	Nok / Greek influence
B.C./A.D. 0				Hellenistic Age	Empire begins: Augustus — emperor	Hengist and Horsa arrived in Kent	Roman invasion / Britain becomes two provinces / Saxons settle			
500 A.D.		Legend: Kupe found New Zealand and told people how to reach there		Empire divided, lands lost. Culture enters new phase	End of Western Roman Empire	England: 12 kingdoms / Athelstan rules all England		Vendel period / Army invade England / Christianity adopted / Viking laws recorded		Kushites' power ends / Arabs settle east coast / Christian European slave trade
1000	Dutch explorers sight Aborigines	Maori arrive / Great Britain annexed New Zealand	Europeans dominate / Cook's voyages / Christianity is introduced			Norman Conquest				
1500	First White settlers									Europeans divide Africa
2000										